The Wicked Wit of
Benjamin
Franklin

The Wicked Wit
of
Benjamin Franklin

*More than 500 Quotes,
Sayings, and Proverbs*

Edited by
MARK SHULMAN

Gramercy Books
New York

For Michael and Martha, & their newfound Marriage:
Love, and be lov'd.
—M.S. 2007

Published by Gramercy Books, an imprint of Random House
Value Publishing, a division of Random House, Inc., New York.

Gramercy is a registered trademark and the colophon is a
trademark of Random House, Inc.

Random House
New York • Toronto • London • Sydney • Auckland
www.valuebooks.com

A catalog record for this title is available from the Library of Congress.

Printed and bound in the United States of America

ISBN: 978-0-517-23080-0

10 9 8 7 6 5 4 3 2 1

Contents

Foreword
by Mark Shulman   VII

The Late Benjamin Franklin
by Mark Twain   I

Introduction to the first *Poor Richard's Almanack* (1733)
by Richard Saunders, and sold by B. Franklin   5

Clean your Finger, before you point at my Spots.
And other Advice for living Well.   II

I saw few die of Hunger, of Eating 100000.
Thoughts Concerning Food, Health, and Death.   19

When Reason preaches, if you won't hear her
she'll box your Ears.
Sage advice on Wisdom, Age, and Education.   27

He that lives upon Hope, dies farting.
Being general Advice for much Self-Improvement.   35

A Penny sav'd is Twopence clear.
The many ways that Money is much misunderstood.   43

There are no fools so troublesome as those that have wit.
A wise examination of Common Foolishnesses.   51

Vice knows she's ugly, so puts on her Mask.
A host of Self-Inflicted troubles, not the Least of
which are Pride and Vanity.   59

Keep Conscience clear, Then never fear.
A dollop of Wisdom for a bushel-full of Happiness.   69

Write Injuries in Dust, Benefits in Marble.
Certain Examples of Friendship, Kindness, and Honour.   75

Keep your eyes wide open before marriage,
half shut afterwards.
Of Love and Marriage, and their After-maths.   85

He that would rise at Court, must begin by Creeping.
A Cross-examination of the Lawyer and His Government.   95

Many have quarrel'd about Religion, that never
practis'd it.
Observations for the Day of Rest and all the rest.   103

Ben beats his Pate, and fancys wit will come;
But he may knock, there's no body at home.
A humble offering of Wit and Humour.   109

Advice on Chusing a Mistress   115

The Drinker's Dictionary   121

The Speech of Miss Polly Baker   127

A Conclusion to *Poor Richard's Almanack*
Also by Richard Saunders   133

Foreword

———◦⊃∞⊂◦———

M EET BENJAMIN FRANKLIN: humorist, scientist, social
scientist, printer, author, philosopher, politician, lover,
thinker, inventor of swim flippers for the hands and other useful items—it's a list that just barely scratches the surface.

Here in this book of wise sayings and keen observations,
you'll find much that Ben Franklin chose to pass along to his
fellow pre-Americans, from the 1730s to the 1750s. But
Franklin himself, the randy libertine, admitted numerous
times that he didn't often live by his own adages. Good advice
is good advice, regardless of whether it's followed.

To make this book helpful as you seek daily advice, each
chapter is a category unto itself. Questions about marriage?
They're answered within. Money concerns? Ben's sage wisdom
will guide you. Friendship? Religion? Health? Yes, yes, yes.

Anything you can think of, Franklin thought of first, and rhym'd. To further benefit you, the quotations are alphabetized within each chapter, thus making it easy to find a quote when you want to use it on someone else.

A Word of Caution: Quote Franklin to each person but few times a day, or soon you may become an unwelcome visitor. In heavy doses on the receiving end, it makes strong medicine.

And now, an introduction to America's best-known humorist from America's other best-known humorist, Mark Twain. In this short essay, Twain found his own ironic means of expressing his sincere gratitude to Benjamin Franklin for creating the unique and unmistakable sound of genuine American writing.

Mark Shulman,
New York City

The Late Benjamin Franklin

by Mark Twain

———◦◦◦———

[Never put off til to-morrow what you can do
day after to-morrow just as well. —B.F.]

T HIS PARTY WAS one of those persons whom they call
Philosophers. He was twins, being born simultaneously in
two different houses in the city of Boston. These houses remain
unto this day, and have signs upon them worded in accordance
with the facts. The signs are considered well enough to have,
though not neccessary, because the inhabitants point out the
two birth-places to the stranger anyhow, and sometimes as often as several times in the same day. The subject of this memoir was of a vicious disposition, and early prostituted his
talents to the invention of maxims and aphorisms calculated to
inflict suffering upon the rising generation of all subsequent
ages. His simplest acts, also, were contrived with a view to
their being held up for the emulation of boys forever—boys
who might otherwise have been happy. It was in this spirit that

he became the son of a soap-boiler; and probably for no other reason than that the efforts of all future boys who tried to be anything might be looked upon with suspicion unless they were the sons of soap-boilers. With a malevolence which is without parallel in history, he would work all day and then sit up nights and let on to be studying algebra by the light of a smouldering fire, so that all other boys might have to do that also or else have Benjamin Franklin thrown up to them. Not satisfied with these proceedings, he had a fashion of living wholly on bread and water, and studying astronomy at meal time—a thing which has brought affliction to millions of boys since, whose fathers had read Franklin's pernicious biography.

His maxims were full of animosity toward boys. Nowadays a boy cannot follow out a single natural instinct without tumbling over some of those everlasting aphorisms and hearing from Franklin on the spot. If he buys two cents worth of peanuts, his father says, "Remember what Franklin has said, my son,—'A groat a day's a penny a year;'" and the comfort is all gone out of those peanuts. If he wants to spin his top when he is done work, his father quotes, "Procrastination is the thief of time." If he does a virtuous action, he never gets anything for it, because "Virtue is its own reward." And that boy is hounded to death and robbed of his natural rest, because Franklin said once in one of his inspired flights of malignity—

Early to bed and early to rise

Make a man healthy and wealthy and wise.

As if it were any object to a boy to be healthy and wealthy and wise on such terms. The sorrow that that maxim has cost me through my parents' experimenting on me with it, tongue cannot tell. The legitimate result is my present state of general debility, indigence, and mental aberration. My parents used to have me up before nine o'clock in the morning, sometimes, when I was a boy. If they had let me take my natural rest, where would I have been now? Keeping store, no doubt, and respected by all.

And what an adroit old adventurer the subject of this memoir was! In order to get a chance to fly his kite on Sunday, he used to hang a key on the string and let on to be fishing for lightning. And a guileless public would go home chirping about the "wisdom" and the "genius" of the hoary Sabbath-breaker. If anybody caught him playing "mumble-peg" by himself, after the age of sixty, he would immediately appear to be ciphering out how the grass grew—as if it was any of his business. My grandfather knew him well, and he says Franklin was always fixed—always ready. If a body, during his old age, happened on him unexpectedly when he was catching flies, or making mud pies, or sliding on a cellar-door, he would immediately look wise, and rip out a maxim, and walk off with his nose in the air and his cap turned wrong side before, trying to appear absent-minded and eccentric. He was a hard lot.

He invented a stove that would smoke your head off in four hours by the clock. One can see the almost devilish satisfaction he took in it, by his giving it his name.

He was always proud of telling how he entered Philadelphia, for the first time, with nothing in the world but two shillings in his pocket and four rolls of bread under his arm. But really, when you come to examine it critically, it was nothing. Anybody could have done it.

To the subject of this memoir belongs the honor of recommending the army to go back to bows and arrows in place of bayonets and muskets. He observed, with his customary force, that the bayonet was very well, under some circumstances, but that he doubted whether it could be used with accuracy at long range.

Benjamin Franklin did a great many notable things for his country, and made her young name to be honored in many lands as the mother of such a son. It is not the idea of this memoir to ignore that or cover it up. No; the simple idea of it is to snub those pretentious maxims of his, which he worked up with a great show of originality out of truisms that had become wearisome platitudes as early as the dispersion from Babel; and also to snub his stove, and his military inspirations, his unseemly endeavor to make himself conspicuous when he entered Philadelphia, and his flying his kite and fooling away his time in all sorts of such ways, when he ought have been foraging for soap-fat, or constructing candles. I merely desired to do away with somewhat of the prevalent calamitous idea among heads of families that Franklin *acquired* his great genius by working for nothing, studying by moonlight, and getting up in the night instead of waiting til morning like a Christian, and that this programme, rigidly inflicted, will make a Franklin of every father's fool. It is time these gentlemen were finding out that these execrable eccentricities of instinct and conduct are only the *evidences* of genius, not the *creators* of it. I wish I had been the father of my parents long enough to make them comprehend this truth, and thus prepare them to let their son have an easier time of it. When I was a child I had to boil soap, notwithstanding my father was wealthy, and I had to get up early and study geometry at breakfast, and peddle my own poetry, and do everything just as Franklin did, in the solemn hope that I would be a Franklin some day. And here I am.

Introduction to the first *Poor Richard's Almanack* (1733)

*by Richard Saunders, Philom. Philadelphia:
Printed and sold by B. Franklin, at the
New Printing-Office near the Market.*

Courteous Reader,

I might in this place attempt to gain thy Favour, by declaring
that I write Almanacks with no other View than that of the
publick Good; but in this I should not be sincere; and Men are
now a-days too wise to be deceiv'd by Pretences how specious
soever. The plain Truth of the Matter is, I am excessive poor,
and my Wife, good Woman, is, I tell her, excessive proud; she
cannot bear, she says, to sit spinning in her Shift of Tow, while
I do nothing but gaze at the Stars; and has threatened more
than once to burn all my Books and Rattling-Traps (as she
calls my Instruments) if I do not make some profitable Use of
them for the good of my Family. The Printer has offer'd me
some considerable share of the Profits, and I have thus begun
to comply with my Dame's desire.

    ... I think my self free to take up the Task, and request a
share of the publick Encourgement; which I am the more apt
to hope for on this Account, that the Buyer of my Almanack
may consider himself, not only as purchasing an useful
Utensil, but as performing an Act of Charity, to his poor
Friend and Servant

R. Saunders

"Mankind are very odd Creatures:
One Half censure what they practise,
the other half practise what they censure;
the rest always say and do as they ought."

Clean your Finger, before you point at my Spots.

And other Advice for living Well.

A new truth is a truth, an old error is an error.

A Slip of the Foot you may soon recover:
But a Slip of the Tongue you may never get over.

A soft Tongue may strike hard.

Ah simple Man! when a boy two precious jewels were given thee, Time, and good Advice; one thou hast lost, and the other thrown away.

An infallible Remedy for the *Tooth-ach,* viz. Wash the Root of an of an aching Tooth, in *Elder Vinegar,* and let it dry half an hour in the Sun; after which it will never ach more; *Probatum est.*

Beware, beware! He'll cheat 'ithout scruple, who can without fear.

Clean your Finger, before you point at my Spots.

Craft must be at charge for clothes, but *Truth* can go naked.

Don't judge of Mens Wealth or Piety, by their *Sunday* Appearance.

Don't think to hunt two hares with one dog.

Don't throw stones at your neighbours, if your own windows are glass.

[13]

Drive thy business; let not that drive thee.

⁓

Force shites upon Reason's Back.

⁓

Graft good Fruit all, or graft not at all.

⁓

He that drinks his Cyder alone, let him catch his Horse alone.

⁓

He that scatters Thorns, let him not go barefoot.

⁓

He that speaks ill of the Mare, will buy her.

⁓

He that won't be counsell'd, can't be help'd.

⁓

Hide not your Talents, they for Use were made.
What's a Sun-Dial in the Shade!

⁓

Honour thy Father and Mother, *i. e.*
Live so as to be an Honour to them tho' they are dead.

⁓

Honours change Manners.

⁓

If evils come not, then our fears are vain:
And if they do, Fear but augments the pain.

⁓

If thou dost ill, the joy fades, not the pains;
If well, the pain doth fade, the joy remains.

⁓

If wind blows on you thro' a hole,
Make your will and take care of your soul.

⁓

If you have no Honey in your Pot, have some in your Mouth.

If you wou'd not be forgotten
As soon as you are dead and rotten,
Either write things worth reading,
Or do things worth the writing.

—

If you'd have your shoes last, put no nails in 'em.

—

If you'd lose a troublesome Visitor, lend him Money.

—

If your head is wax, don't walk in the Sun.

—

Ill Customs & bad Advice are seldom forgotten.

—

It is better to take many Injuries than to give one.

—

Late Children, early Orphans.

—

Light Gains heavy Purses.

—

Little Strokes,
Fell great Oaks.

—

Make haste slowly.

—

Neglect mending a small Fault, and 'twill soon be a great One.

—

Never intreat a servant to swell with thee.

—

Never spare the Parson's wine, nor the Baker's pudding.

—

Not to oversee Workmen, is to leave them your Purse open.

Plough deep, while Sluggards sleep;
And you shall have Corn, to sell and to keep.

—

Proclaim not all thou knowest, all thou owest, all thou hast,
nor all thou canst.

—

Quarrels never could last long,
If on one side only lay the wrong.

—

Rob not for burnt offerings.

—

Sell not virtue to purchase wealth, nor Liberty to purchase
power.

—

She who attacks another's Honour
Draws every living Thing upon her.
Think, Madam, when you stretch your Lungs,
That all your Neighbours too have Tongues;
One Slander fifty will beget;
The World with Interest pays the Debt.

—

Sin is not hurtful because it is forbidden but it is forbidden
because it's hurtful. Nor is a Duty beneficial because it is
commanded, but it is commanded, because it's beneficial.

—

Speak and speed: the close mouth catches no flies.

—

Take counsel in wine, but resolve afterwards in water.

—

The ancients tell us what is best;
But we must learn of the moderns what is fittest.

The Honey is sweet, but the Bee has a Sting.

—

There's a time to wink as well as to see.

—

There's none deceived but he that trusts.

—

Thirst after Desert, not Reward.

—

Time enough, always proves *little enough.*

—

Tis easy to see, hard to foresee.

—

To be *proud* of *Knowledge,* is to be *blind* with *Light*;
to be *proud* of *Virtue,* is to *poison* yourself with the
Antidote.

—

To Friend, Lawyer, Doctor, tell plain your whole Case;
Nor think on bad Matters to put a good Face:
How can they advise, if they see but a Part?
'Tis very ill driving black Hogs in the dark.

—

Visit your Aunt, but not every Day; and call at your Brother's,
but not every night.

—

Want of Care does us more Damage than Want of Knowledge.

—

When you speak to a man, look on his eyes; when he speaks to
thee, look on his mouth.

—

When you're an Anvil, hold you still;
When you're a Hammer, strike your Fill.

[17]

Who is wise? He that learns from every One.
Who is powerful? He that governs his Passions.
Who is rich? He that is content.
Who is that? Nobody.

⌒

Who says Jack is not generous? He is always fond of giving,
and cares not for receiving.
—What? Why; Advice.

⌒

Wide will wear, but Narrow will tear.

⌒

With the old Almanack and the old Year,
Leave thy old Vices, tho' ever so dear.

⌒

Wouldst thou confound thine Enemy, be good thy self.

⌒

You will be careful, if you are wise;
How you touch Men's Religion, or Credit, or Eyes.

I saw few die of Hunger, of Eating 100000.

Thoughts Concerning Food, Health, and Death.

A full Belly makes a dull Brain:
The Muses starve in a Cook's Shop.

Against Diseases here, the strongest Fence,
Is the defensive Virtue, Abstinence.

Cheese and salt meat, should be sparingly eat.

Death is a Fisherman, the world we see
His Fish-pond is, and we the Fishes be:
His Net some general Sickness; howe'er he
Is not so kind as other Fishers be;
For if they take one of the smaller Fry,
They throw him in again, he shall not die:
But Death is sure to kill all he can get,
And all is Fish with him that comes to Net.

Death takes no bribes.

Dine with little, sup with less:
Do better still; sleep supperless.

Drink Water, Put the Money in your Pocket, and leave the
Dry-*bellyach* in the *Punchbowl.*

Eat and drink such an exact Quantity as the Constitution of
thy Body allows of, in reference to the Services of the Mind.

Eat to live, and not live to eat.

Eat to please thyself, but dress to please others.

[21]

Fear not Death; for the sooner we die, the longer shall we be immortal.

—

Finikin *Dick*, curs'd with nice Taste,
Ne'er meets with good dinner, half starv'd at a feast.

—

God heals, and the Doctor takes the Fees.

—

He that can travel well afoot, keeps a good horse.

—

He that lives carnally, won't live eternally.

—

He that never eats too much, will never be lazy.

—

He's the best physician that knows the worthlessness of the most medicines.

—

Hold your Council before Dinner; the full Belly hates Thinking as well as Acting.

—

Hot things, sharp things, sweet things, cold things
All rot the teeth, and make them look like old things.

Hunger is the best Pickle.

—

I saw few die of Hunger, of Eating 100000.

—

If it were not for the Belly, the Back might wear Gold.

—

If thou art dull and heavy after Meat, it's a sign thou hast exceeded the due Measure; for Meat and Drink ought to refresh the Body, and make it chearful, and not to dull and oppress it.

In Life's more tedious Journey, Man delays
T'enquire out the Number of his Days:
He cares, not he, how slow his Hours spend,
The Journey's better than the Journey's End.

———

Keep out of the Sight of Feasts and Banquets as much as may
be; for 'tis more difficult to refrain good Cheer, when it's present, than from the Desire of it when it is away; the like you
may observe in the Objects of all the other Senses.

———

Keep your mouth wet, feet dry.

———

Lord, if our Days be *few,* why do we spend,
And lavish them to such an evil End?
Or, why, if they be *evil,* do we wrong
Our selves and thee, in wishing them so long?
Our Days decrease, our evils still renew,
We make them *ill,* thou kindly mak'st them *few.*

———

Many a Meal is lost for want of meat.

———

Many dishes many diseases,
Many medicines few cures.

———

Men drop so fast, ere Life's mid Stage we tread,
Few know so many Friends *alive* as *dead* ...

———

No wonder *Tom* grows fat, th' unwieldy Sinner,
Makes his whole Life but one continual Dinner.

———

Onions can make ev'n heirs and Widows weep.

———

Pain wastes the Body, Pleasures the Understanding.

Poor Dick, eats like a well man, and drinks like a sick.

———

Take Courage, Mortal; Death can't banish thee out of the Universe.

———

The Difficulty lies, in finding out an exact Measure; but eat for Necessity, not Pleasure, for Lust knows not where Necessity ends.

———

The poor man must walk to get meat for his stomach, the rich man to get a stomach to his meat.

———

They that study much, ought not to eat so much as those that work hard, their Digestion being not so good.

———

Three good meals a day is a bad living.

———

Tim moderate fare and abstinence much prizes,
In publick, but in private gormandizes.

———

To lengthen thy Life, lessen thy Meals.

———

Too much plenty makes Mouth dainty.

———

What Death is, dost thou ask of me;
 Till dead I do not know;
Come to me when thou hear'st I'm dead;
 Then what 'tis I shall show.
To die's to cease to be, it seems,
 So Learned Seneca did think;
But we've Philosophers of modern Date,
Who say 'tis Death to cease to Drink.

When Death puts out our Flame, the Snuff will tell,
If we were Wax, or Tallow by the Smell.

⁓

Whimsical Will once fancy'd he was ill,
The Doctor's call'd, who thus examin'd Will;
How is your Appetite? O, as to that
I eat right heartily, you see I'm fat.
How is your Sleep anights? 'Tis sound and good;
I eat, drink, sleep as well as e'er I cou'd.
Well, says the Doctor, clapping on his Hat;
I'll give you something shall remove all that.

⁓

Wouldst thou enjoy a long Life, a healthy Body, and a vigor-
ous Mind, and be acquainted also with the wonderful works of
God? labour in the first place to bring thy Appetite into
Subjection to Reason.

When Reason preaches, if you won't hear her she'll box your Ears.

Sage advice on Wisdom, Age, and Education.

A Change of *Fortune* hurts a wise Man no more than a Change of the *Moon*.

A fine genius in his own country, is like gold in the mine.

A Man of Knowledge like a rich Soil, feeds
If not a world of Corn, a world of Weeds.

A taught horse, and a woman to teach,
And teachers practicing what they preach.

A wise Man will desire no more, than what he may get justly, use soberly, distribute chearfully, and leave contentedly.

After crosses and losses men grow humbler & wiser.

Altho' thy Teacher act not as he preaches,
Yet ne'ertheless, if good, do what he teaches;
Good Counsel, failing Men may give; for why,
He that's aground knows where the Shoal doth lie.

An ounce of wit that is bought,
Is worth a pound that is taught.

As for old Age, 'twill be incurable this Year, because of the Years past.

At 20 years of age the Will reigns; at 30 the Wit; at 40 the Judgment.

Be temperate in wine, in eating, girls, and sloth;
Or the Gout will seize you and plague you both.

—

Beware of the young Doctor & the old Barber.

—

Blessed is he that expects nothing, for he shall never be
disappointed.

—

By nought is Man from Beast distinguished
More than by Knowledge in his learned Head.
Then Youth improve thy Time, but cautious see
That what thou learnest some how useful be.
Each Day improving, Solon waxed old;
For Time he knew was better far than Gold:
Fortune might give him Gold which would decay,
But Fortune cannot give him Yesterday.

—

Can grave and formal pass for wise,
When Men the solemn Owl despise?

—

Cold and cunning come from the north:
But cunning sans wisdom is nothing worth.

—

Distrust & caution are the parents of security.

—

Do not do that which you would not have known.

—

Don't go to the doctor with every distemper,
Nor to the lawyer with every quarrel,
Nor to the pot for every thirst.

—

Fools make feasts and wise men eat 'em.

Fools need Advice most, but wise Men only are the better for it.

⁓

For Age and Want save while you may;
No Morning Sun lasts a whole Day.

⁓

Genius without Education is like Silver in the Mine.

⁓

Good Sense is a Thing all need, few have, and none think they want.

⁓

He that best understands the World, least likes it.

⁓

He that can bear a Reproof, and mend by it, if he is not wise, is in a fair way of being so.

⁓

He that can compose himself, is wiser than he that composes books.

⁓

He that cannot bear with other People's Passions, cannot govern his own.

⁓

He that knows nothing of it, may by chance be a Prophet;
While the wisest that is may happen to miss.

⁓

He that lives well, is learned enough.

⁓

He that pursues two Hares at once, does not catch one and lets t'other go.

⁓

He that would live in peace & at ease, Must not speak all he knows, nor judge all he sees.

Hear *Reason,* or she'll make you feel her.

—

Historians relate, not so much what is done, as what they would have believed.

—

If thou hast wit & learning,
Add to it Wisdom and Modesty.

—

If thou wouldst live long, live well; for Folly and Wickedness shorten Life.

—

It is wise not to seek a Secret, and Honest not to reveal it.

—

Keep flax from fire, and youth from gaming.

—

Let thy Child's first Lesson be Obedience, and the second may be what thou wilt.

—

Life with Fools consists in Drinking;
With the wise Man Living's Thinking.

—

Many Foxes grow grey, but few grow good.

—

Most of the Learning in use, is of no great Use.

—

Old Boys have their Playthings as well as young Ones;
the Difference is only in the Price.

—

Old young and old long.

—

Since I cannot govern my own tongue, tho' within my own teeth, how can I hope to govern the tongues of others?

Some are weatherwise, some are otherwise.

—

Teach your child to hold his tongue, he'l learn fast enough to speak.

—

The cunning man steals a horse,
the wise man lets him alone.

—

The excellency of hogs is fatness, of men virtue.

—

The Golden Age never was the present Age.

—

The heart of a fool is in his mouth, but the mouth of a wise man is in his heart.

—

The Master's Eye will do more Work than both his Hands.

—

The wise Man draws more Advantage from his Enemies, than the Fool from his Friends.

—

There have been as great Souls unknown to fame as any of the most famous.

—

Thou hadst better eat salt with the Philosophers of *Greece*, than sugar with the Courtiers of *Italy*.

—

Time eateth all things, could old Poets say;
The Times are chang'd, our times drink all away.

—

To-day is Yesterday's Pupil.

—

To-morrow I'll reform, the Fool does say:
To day it self's too late; the Wise did yesterday.

Weighty Questions ask for deliberate Answers.

When Reason preaches,
if you won't hear her she'll box your Ears.

When the Well's dry, we know the Worth of Water.

When the Wine enters, out goes the Truth.

Wise Men learn by others harms; Fools by their own.

Write with the learned, pronounce with the vulgar.

Youth is pert and positive, *Age* modest and doubting: So Ears of Corn when young and light, stand bolt upright, but hang their Heads when weighty, full, and ripe.

He that lives upon Hope, dies farting.

Being general advice for much Self-Improvement.

Who is strong? He that can conquer his bad Habits.
Who is rich? He that rejoices in his Portion.

'Tis easier to suppress the first Desire,
than to satisfy all that follow.

'Tis easier to prevent bad habits than to break them.

A good Example is the best sermon.

A Man without ceremony has need of great merit in its place.

A Traveller should have a hog's nose, deer's legs, and an ass's back.

An Egg to day is better than a Hen to-morrow.

An ill Wound, but not an ill Name, may be healed.

As we must account for every idle word, so we must for every idle silence.

Be neither silly, nor cunning, but wise.

Cesar did not merit the triumphal Car,
more than he that conquers himself.

Courage would fight, but Discretion won't let him.

Defer not thy well doing; be not like *St. George*, who is always a horseback, and never rides on.

—

Deny Self for Self's sake.

—

Diligence is the mother of Good-Luck.

—

Diligence overcomes Difficulties, Sloth makes them.

—

Dost thou love Life? Then do not squander Time; for that's the Stuff Life is made of.

—

Each year one vicious habit rooted out,
In time might make the worst Man good throughout.

—

Early to bed and early to rise, makes a man healthy, wealthy and wise.

—

Fear to do ill, and you need fear nought else.

—

For want of a Nail the Shoe is lost;
For want of a Shoe, the Horse is lost;
For want of a Horse the Rider is lost.

—

Glass, China, and Reputation, are easily crack'd, and never well mended.

—

God helps them that help themselves.

—

Great Beauty, great strength, & great Riches, are really & truly of no great Use; a right Heart exceeds all.

—

Great Modesty often hides great Merit.

[38]

Great Talkers, little Doers.

⁓

Hast thou virtue? acquire also the graces & beauties of virtue.

⁓

Haste makes Waste.

⁓

He that can have Patience,
can have what he will.

⁓

He that lives upon Hope, dies farting.

⁓

He that resolves to mend hereafter, resolves not to mend now.

⁓

He that riseth late, must trot all day, and shall scarce overtake
his business at night.

⁓

He that speaks much, is much mistaken.

⁓

Humility makes great men twice honourable.

⁓

Idleness is the greatest Prodigality.

⁓

If you have time don't wait for time.

⁓

If you wou'd be reveng'd of your enemy, govern your self.

⁓

If you'd have it done, Go: If not, send.

⁓

If you'd have a Servant that you like, serve your self.

⁓

In a corrupt Age, the putting the World in order would breed
Confusion; then e'en mind your own Business.

[39]

Industry, Perseverance, and Frugality, make Fortune yield.

Let our Fathers and Grandfathers be valued for *their* Goodness, ourselves for our own.

Let thy vices die before thee.

Look before, or you'll find yourself behind.

Lost Time is never found again.

Many a Man would have been worse, if his Estate had been better.

Many complain of their memory, few of their Judgment.

No gains without pains.

None preaches better than the ant, and she says nothing.

O Lazy-Bones! Dost thou think God would have given thee Arms and Legs, if he had not design'd thou should'st use them.

Observe all men; thy self most.

Pride and the Gout,
Are seldom cur'd throughout.

Prosperity discovers Vice, Adversity Virtue.

Read much, but not many Books.

Reading makes a full Man, Meditation a profound Man, discourse a clear Man.

—

Search others for their virtues, thy self for thy vices.

—

Seek Virtue, and, of that possest,
To Providence, resign the rest.

—

Setting too good an Example is a Kind of Slander seldom forgiven; 'tis *Scandalum Magnatum.*

—

Since thou art not sure of a minute, throw not away an hour.

—

Sloth (like Rust) consumes faster than Labour wears: the used Key is always bright.

—

Taxes are indeed very heavy, and if those laid on by the Government were the only Ones we had to pay, we might more easily discharge them; but we have many others, and much more grievous to some of us. We are taxed twice as much by our Idleness, three times as much by our Pride, and four times as much by our Folly, and from these Taxes the Commissioners cannot ease or deliver us by allowing an Abatement.

—

The busy Man has few idle Visitors; to the boiling Pot the Flies come not.

—

The Sting of a Reproach, is the Truth of it.

—

The Things which hurt, instruct.

—

There are three Things extremely hard: Steel, a Diamond, and to know one's self.

There is much difference between imitating a good man, and counterfeiting him.

To God we owe fear and love; to our neighbours justice and charity; to our selves prudence and sobriety.

To-morrow, every Fault is to be amended; but that *To-morrow* never comes.

What one relishes, nourishes.

What you would seem to be, be really.

When 'tis fair be sure take your Great coat with you.

When out of Favour, none know thee; when in, thou dost not know thyself.

Who judges best of a Man, his Enemies or himself?

Wink at small faults; remember thou hast great ones.

Women & Wine, Game & Deceit,
Make the Wealth small and the Wants great.

Words may shew a man's Wit, but *Actions* his Meaning.

Would you persuade, speak of Interest, not of Reason.

Write with the learned, pronounce with the vulgar.

A Penny sav'd is Twopence clear

The many ways that Money is
much misunderstood.

A light purse is a heavy Curse.

A Penny sav'd is Twopence clear,
A Pin a day is a Groat a Year.

All things are cheap to the saving, dear to the wasteful.

Among the Divines there has been much Debate,
Concerning the World in its ancient Estate;
Some say 'twas once good, but now is grown bad,
Some say 'tis reform'd of the Faults it once had:
I say, 'tis the best World, this that we now live in,
Either to lend, or to spend, or to give in;
But to borrow, to beg, or to get a Man's own,
It is the worst World that ever was known.

At a great Pennyworth, pause a while.

Bargaining has neither friends nor relations.

Beware of little Expences, a small Leak will sink a great Ship.

Buy what thou hast no need of;
And e'er long thou shalt sell thy necessaries.

Creditors have better memories than debtors.

For one poor Man there are an hundred indigent.

Great spenders are bad lenders.

[45]

He does not possess Wealth, it possesses him.

⁓

He that buys by the penny, maintains not only himself, but other people.

⁓

He that buys upon Credit, pays Interest for what he buys. And he that pays ready Money, might let that Money out to Use, so that He that possesses any Thing he has bought, pays Interest for the Use of it.

⁓

He that by the Plow would thrive,
Himself must either hold or drive.

⁓

He that drinks fast, pays slow.

⁓

He that is of Opinion Money will do every Thing, may well be suspected of doing every Thing for Money.

⁓

He that is rich need not live sparingly, and he that can live sparingly need not be rich.

⁓

He that loses 5s [shillings] not only loses that Sum, but all the Advantage that might be made by turning it in Dealing, which by the time that a young Man becomes old, amounts to a comfortable Bag of Mony.

⁓

He that pays for Work before it's done, has but a pennyworth for twopence.

⁓

He that sells upon trust, loses many friends, and always wants money.

He that would have a short Lent, let him borrow Money to be repaid at Easter.

He's a Fool that makes his Doctor his Heir.

He's gone, and forgot nothing but to say *Farewel*—to his creditors.

I have never seen the Philosopher's Stone that turns lead into Gold, but I have known the pursuit of it turn a Man's Gold into Lead.

If you'd be wealthy, think of saving, more than of getting.

If you'd know the Value of Money, go and borrow some.

If your Riches are yours, why don't you take them with you to the t'other World?

Impudent Jack, who now lives by his Shifts,
Borrowing of Driblets, boldly begging Gifts;
For Twenty Shillings lent him t'other Day
(By one who ne'er expected he would pay)
On his Friend's Paper fain a Note wou'd write;
His Friend, as needless, did refuse it quite;
Paper was scarce, and 'twas too hard, it's true,
To part with Cash, and lose his Paper too.

Lend Money to an Enemy, and thou'lt gain him, to a Friend and thou'lt lose him.

Liberality is not giving much but giving wisely.

[47]

Light purse, heavy heart.

⁓

Lying rides upon Debt's back.

⁓

Money and Man a mutual Friendship show:
Man makes *false* Money, Money makes Man so.

⁓

Neither trust, nor contend, nor lay wagers, nor lend;
And you'll have peace to your Lives end.

⁓

Nothing but Money,
Is Sweeter than Honey.

⁓

Now I've a sheep and a cow,
Every body bids me good morrow.

⁓

Patience in Market, is worth Pounds in a Year.

⁓

Pay what you owe, and what you're worth you'll know.

⁓

Pay what you owe, and you'll know what's your own.

⁓

Poverty wants some things, Luxury many things, Avarice all
things.

⁓

Rather go to bed supperless, than run in debt for a Breakfast.

⁓

Receive before you write, but write before you pay.

⁓

Save & have.

⁓

Sleep without Supping, and you'll rise without owing for it.

Some are justly laught at for keeping their Money foolishly, others for spending it idly: He is the greatest fool that lays it out in a purchase of repentance.

The *Borrower* is a Slave to the *Lender*; the *Security* to *both*.

The creditors are a superstitious sect, great observers of set days and times.

The good Paymaster is Lord of another man's Purse.

The misers cheese is the wholesomest.

The poor have little, beggars none, the rich too much, *enough* not one.

The second Vice is lying; the first is Running in Debt.

The thrifty maxim of the wary *Dutch*, is to save all the Money they can touch.

The Use of Money is all the Advantage there is in having Money.

'Tis against some Mens Principle to pay Interest, and seems against others Interest to pay the Principal.

'Tis hard (but glorious) to be poor and honest: An empty Sack can hardly stand upright; but if it does, 'tis a stout one!

Virtue was reckon'd the chief Thing of Old;
Now lies all Merit in Silver and Gold:
Virtue has lost its Regard in these Times,
While Money, like Charity, covers all Crimes.

[49]

When other Sins grow old by Time,
Then Avarice is in its prime,
Yet feed the Poor at *Christmas* time.

When *Prosperity* was well mounted, she let go the Bridle, and soon came tumbling out of the Saddle.

Wish a miser long life, and you wish him no good.

There are no fools so troublesome as those that have wit.

A wise examination of Common Foolishnesses.

A Child thinks 20 *Shillings* and 20 Years can scarce ever be spent.

A great Talker may be no Fool, but he is one that relies on him.

A learned blockhead is a greater blockhead than an ignorant one.

A Man in a Passion rides a mad Horse.

A man is never so ridiculous by those Qualities that are his own as by those that he affects to have.

Anger is never without a Reason; but seldom with a good One.

Bad Commentators spoil the best of books,
So God sends meat (they say) the devil Cooks.

Being ignorant is not so much a Shame, as being unwilling to learn.

Blame-all and *Praise-all* are two blockheads.

Children and Princes will quarrel for Trifles.

Doors and walls are fools paper.

Empty Free-booters, cover'd with Scorn:
They went out for Wealth, and come ragged and torn,
As the Ram went for Wool, and was sent back shorn.

Ever since Follies have pleas'd,
Fools have been able to divert.

—

Every Man has Assurance enough to boast of his honesty, few of their Understanding.

—

Experience keeps a dear school, yet Fools will learn in no other.

—

Fools make feasts and wise men eat them.

—

Fools multiply folly.

—

Half Wits talk much but say little.

—

He has chang'd his one ey'd horse for a blind one.

—

He is no clown that drives the plow, but he that doth clownish things.

—

He is not well-bred, that cannot bear Ill-Breeding in others.

—

He that falls in love with himself, will have no Rivals.

—

He that whines for Glass without G
Take away L and that's he.

—

He's a Fool that cannot conceal his Wisdom.

—

Here comes the Orator! with his Flood of Words, and his Drop of Reason.

—

It is Ill-Manners to silence a Fool, and Cruelty to let him go on.

It's the easiest Thing in the World for a Man to
deceive himself.

⌒

Many a Man's own Tongue gives Evidence against his
Understanding.

⌒

Most Fools think they are only ignorant.

⌒

Never mind it, she'l be sober after the Holidays.

⌒

Nick's Passions grow fat and hearty; his Understanding looks
consumptive!

⌒

None are deceived but they that confide.

⌒

Nothing more like a Fool, than a drunken Man.

⌒

Of learned Fools I have seen ten times ten,

⌒

Of unlearned wise men I have seen a hundred.

Pollio, who values nothing that's within,
Buys Books as men hunt Beavers,—for their Skin.

⌒

Presumption first blinds a Man, then sets him a running.

⌒

Relation without friendship, friendship without power, power
without will, will witho. effect, effect without profit, & profit
without vertue, are not worth a farto.

⌒

Sloth and Silence are a Fool's Virtues.

Strange! that a Man who has wit enough to write a Satyr; should have folly enough to publish it.

—

The absent are never without fault, nor the present without excuse.

—

The family of Fools is ancient.

—

The first Degree of Folly, is to conceit one's self wise; the second to profess it; the third to despise Counsel.

—

The fool hath made a vow, I guess,
Never to let the Fire have peace.

—

The hasty Bitch brings forth blind Puppies.

—

The learned Fool writes his Nonsense in better Language than the unlearned; but still 'tis Nonsense.

—

The most exquisite Folly is made of Wisdom spun too fine.

—

The old Man has given all to his Son:
O fool! to undress thy self before thou art going to bed.

—

There are lazy Minds as well as lazy Bodies.

—

There are no fools so troublesome as those that have wit.

—

There is much money given to be laught at, though the purchasers don't know it; witness *A's* fine horse, & *B's* fine house.

—

There's many witty men whose brains can't fill their bellies.

Tim was so learned, that he could name a Horse in nine Languages; So ignorant, that he bought a Cow to ride on.

＊

To all apparent Beauties blind
Each Blemish strikes an envious Mind.

＊

To be intimate with a foolish Friend, is like going to bed to a Razor.

＊

Two Faults of one a Fool will make;
He half repairs, that owns and does forsake.

＊

Where Sense is wanting, every thing is wanting.

＊

Who has deceiv'd thee so oft as thy self?

＊

Who knows a fool, must know his brother;
For one will recommend another.

＊

You may talk too much on the best of subjects.

Vice knows she's ugly, so puts on her Mask.

A host of Self-Inflicted troubles,
not the Least of which
are Pride and Vanity.

A Flatterer never seems absurd:
The Flatter'd always take his Word.

—

A full Belly brings forth every Evil.

—

A good Man is seldom uneasy, an ill one never easie.

—

A large train makes a light Purse.

—

A quiet Conscience sleeps in Thunder,
But Rest and Guilt live far asunder.

—

A rich rogue, is like a fat hog,
who never does good til as dead as a log.

—

A Temper to bear much, will have much to bear.

—

A wicked Hero will turn his back to an innocent coward.

—

Admiration is the Daughter of Ignorance.

—

Ambition often spends foolishly what *Avarice* had wickedly
collected.

—

Anger is never without a Reason, but seldom with a good One.

—

Anoint a villain and he'll stab you, stab him & he'l anoint you.

—

Approve not of him who commends all you say.

Are you angry that others disappoint you? remember you cannot depend upon yourself.

———

As Charms are nonsense,
Nonsence is a Charm.

———

As Pride increases, Fortune declines.

———

As sore places meet most rubs, proud folks meet most affronts.

———

Bad Gains are truly Losses.

———

Beauty & Folly are old companions.

———

Beware of him that is slow to anger: He is angry for something, and will not be pleased for nothing.

———

Beware of meat twice boil'd, and an old Foe reconcil'd.

———

Changing Countries or Beds, cures neither a bad Manager, nor a Fever.

———

Cunning proceeds from Want of Capacity.

———

Danger is Sauce for Prayers.

———

Declaiming against Pride, is not always a Sign of Humility.

———

Despair ruins some, Presumption many.

———

Don't think so much of your own Cunning, as to forget other Mens: A cunning Man is overmatch'd by a cunning Man and a Half.

Fair Decency, celestial Maid,
Descend from Heav'n to Beauty's Aid:
Tho' Beauty may beget Desire,
'Tis thou must fan the Lover's Fire:
For, Beauty, like supreme Dominion,
Is best supported by Opinion:
If Decency bring no Supplies,
Opinion falls and Beauty dies.

Fond Pride of Dress is sure an empty Curse;
E're *Fancy* you consult, consult your Purse.

From a cross Neighbour, and a sullen Wife,
A pointless Needle, and a broken Knife;
From Suretyship, and from an empty Purse,
A Smoaky Chimney and a jolting Horse;
From a dull Razor, and an aking Head,
From a bad Conscience and a buggy Bed;
A Blow upon the Elbow and the Knee,
From each of these, *Good L—d deliver me*.

Full of courtesie, full of craft.

Great famine when wolves eat wolves.

Great Pride and Meanness sure are near ally'd;
Or thin Partitions do their Bounds divide.

Having been poor is no shame, but being ashamed of it, is.

He that carries a small Crime easily, will carry it on when it comes to be an Ox.

He that hath no *ill* Fortune will be troubled with *good*.

[63]

He that lies down with Dogs, shall rise up with fleas.

He that sows Thorns, should never go barefoot.

Hunger never saw bad bread.

If Man could have Half his Wishes, he would double his Troubles.

If Pride leads the Van,
Beggary brings up the Rear.

If what most men admire, they would despise,
'Twould look as if mankind were growing wise.

If you do what you should not, you must hear what you would not.

In other men we faults can spy,
And blame the mote that dims their eye;
Each little speck and blemish find;
To our own stronger errors blind.

It's common for Men to give 6 pretended Reasons instead of one real one.

Knaves and Nettles are akin;
Stroak 'em kindly, yet they'll sting.

Laziness travels so slowly, that Poverty soon overtakes him.

Meanness is the Parent of Insolence.

Necessity never made a good bargain.

Neglect kills Injuries, Revenge increases them.

None know the unfortunate, and the fortunate do not know themselves.

Nothing exceeds in Ridicule, no doubt,
A Fool *in* Fashion, but a Fool that's *out;*
His Passion for Absurdity's so strong
He cannot bear a Rival in the Wrong.
Tho' wrong the Mode, comply; more Sense is shewn
In wearing others Follies than your own.

If what is out of Fashion most you prize,
Methinks you should endeavour to be wise.

One Man may be more cunning than another, but not more cunning than every body else.

One Mend-fault is worth two Findfaults, but one Findfault is better than two Makefaults.

Paintings and Fightings are best seen at a distance.

Pardoning the Bad, is injuring the Good.

Poverty, Poetry and new Titles of Honour, make Men ridiculous.

Pox take you, is no curse to some people.

Pray don't burn my House to roast your Eggs.

Pride breakfasted with *Plenty*, dined with *Poverty*, supped with *Infamy*.

Pride gets into the Coach, and *Shame* mounts behind.

—

Pride is as loud a Beggar as *Want,* and a great deal more saucy.

Pride is said to be the *last* vice the good man gets clear of.

—

Saying and Doing, have quarrel'd and parted.

—

Shame and the *Dry-belly-ach* were Diseases of the last Age; this seems to be cured of them.

—

She that paints her face, thinks of her Tail.

—

Some of our Sparks to London town do go
Fashions to see, and learn the World to know;
Who at Return have nought but these to show,
New Wig above, and new Disease below.
Thus the Jack Ass a Traveller once would be,
And roam'd abroad new Fashions for to see;
But home returned, Fashions he had none,
Only his Main and Tail were larger grown.

—

Sorrow is good for nothing but Sin.

—

Suspicion may be no Fault, but shewing it may be a great one.

—

Take this remark from Richard poor and lame,
Whate'er's begun in anger ends in shame.

—

The Devil sweetens Poison with Honey.

—

The favour of the Great is no inheritance.

—

The honest Man takes Pains, and then enjoys Pleasures; the Knave takes Pleasure, and then suffers Pains.

[66]

The Proud hate Pride—in others.

The too obliging Temper is evermore disobliging itself.

The Wolf sheds his Coat once a Year, his Disposition never.

There is neither honour nor gain, got in dealing with a vil-lain.

There is no little enemy.

There is no Man so bad, but he secretly respects the Good.

There was never a good Knife made of bad Steel.

There's small Revenge in Words, but Words may be greatly revenged.

Those that have much Business must have much Pardon.

Those who are fear'd, are hated.

'Tis a Shame that your Family is an Honour to you! You ought to be an Honour to your Family.

Tongue double, brings trouble.

Trouble springs from *Idleness*; *Toil* from *Ease*.

Two dry Sticks will burn a green One.

Vain-Glory flowereth, but beareth no Fruit.

Vanity backbites more than *Malice*.

Vice knows she's ugly, so puts on her Mask.

[67]

Virtue may not always make a Face handsome, but *Vice* will
certainly make it ugly.

⸺

Welcome, Mischief, if thou comest alone.

⸺

What is a butterfly? At best
He's but a caterpiller drest.

⸺

The gaudy Fop's his picture just.

⸺

What maintains one Vice would bring up two Children.

⸺

What pains our Justice takes his faults to hide,
With half that pains sure he might cure 'em quite.

⸺

What will not Lux'ry taste? Earth, Sea, and Air,
Are daily ransack'd for the Bill of Fare.

⸺

What's Beauty? Call ye that your own,
A Flow'r that fades as soon as blown!
Those Eyes of so divine a Ray,
What are they? Mould'ring, mortal Clay.
Those Features cast in heav'nly Mould,
Shall, like my coarser Earth, grow old;
Like common Grass, the fairest Flow'r
Must feel the hoary Season's Pow'r.

⸺

When Knaves betray each other, one can scarce be blamed, or
the other pitied.

⸺

Where bread is wanting, all's to be sold.

⸺

Why does the blind man's wife paint herself?

⸺

You may be too cunning for One, but not for All.

[68]

Keep Conscience clear, Then never fear.

A dollop of Wisdom for
a bushel-full of Happiness.

A fat kitchin, a lean Will.

A little House well fill'd, a little Field well till'd, and a little Wife well will'd, are great Riches.

A long Life may not be good enough, but a good Life is long enough.

A Man has no more *Goods* than he gets Good by.

Act uprightly, and despise Calumny; Dirt may stick to a Mud Wall, but not to polish'd Marble.

Avarice and Happiness never saw each other, how then shou'd they become acquainted.

Better is a little with content than much with contention.

Content and Riches seldom meet together,
Riches take thou, contentment I had rather.

Content is the Philosopher's Stone, that turns all it touches into Gold.

Content makes poor men rich; Discontent makes rich Men poor.

Doing an Injury puts you below your Enemy; *Revenging* one makes you but *even* with him; *Forgiving* it sets you *above* him.

Don't misinform your Doctor nor your Lawyer.

—

Drink does not drown *Care,* but waters it, and makes it grow faster.

—

Fly Pleasures, and they'll follow you.

—

Gifts much expected, are *paid*, not *given*.

—

Grace then thy House, and let not that grace thee.

—

Great-Alms-giving, lessens no Man's Living.

—

Great Estates may venture more;
Little Boats must keep near Shore.

—

He that can take rest is greater than he that can take cities.

—

He that's content, hath enough; He that complains, has too much.

—

He who multiplies Riches multiplies Cares.

—

Hope of gain lessens pain.

—

If thou injurest Conscience, it will have its Revenge on thee.

—

If you desire many things, many things will seem but a few.

—

If you know how to spend less than you get, you have the Philosophers-Stone.

If you'd be belov'd, make yourself amiable.

—

Is there any thing Men take more pains about than to render themselves unhappy?

—

Keep Conscience clear,
Then never fear.

—

Let no Pleasure tempt thee, no Profit allure thee, no Ambition corrupt thee, no Example sway thee, no Persuasion move thee, to do any thing which thou knowest to be Evil; So shalt thou always live jollily; for a good Conscience is a continual Christmas.

—

Let thy discontents be thy Secrets; if the world knows them, 'twill despise *thee* and increase them.

—

Let thy maidservant be faithful, strong, and homely.

—

Many a Man thinks he is buying Pleasure, when he is really selling himself a Slave to it.

—

Nice Eaters seldom meet with a good Dinner.

—

Nothing brings more pain than too much pleasure; nothing more bondage than too much liberty, (or libertinism.)

—

The discontented Man finds no easy Chair.

—

The Master-piece of Man, is to live to the purpose.

—

They who have nothing to be troubled at, will be troubled at nothing.

Wealth and Content are not always Bedfellows.

Wealth is not his that has it, but his that enjoys it.

Who pleasure gives, Shall joy receive.

Would you live with ease,
Do what you ought, and not what you please.

Write Injuries in Dust, Benefits in Marble.

Certain Examples of Friendship, Kindness, and Honour.

A false Friend and a Shadow, attend only while the Sun shines.

A Father's a Treasure; a Brother's a Comfort; a Friend is both.

A lie stands on 1 leg, Truth on 2.

A true friend is the best Possession.

A true great Man will neither trample on a Worm, nor sneak to an Emperor.

After 3 days men grow weary, of a wench, a guest, & weather rainy.

An open Foe may prove a curse;
But a pretended friend is worse.

A wolf eats sheep but now and then,
Ten Thousands are devour'd by Men.
Man's tongue is soft, and bone doth lack;
Yet a stroke therewith may break a man's back.

As often as we do good, we sacrifice.

Ask and have, is sometimes dear buying.

Be civil to *all*; serviceable to *many*; familiar with *few*; Friend to *one*; Enemy to *none*.

Be good to thy Friend to keep him, to thy enemy to gain him.

Be not niggardly of what costs thee nothing, as courtesy, counsel, & countenance.

—

Be slow in chusing a Friend, slower in changing.

—

Beware of meat twice boil'd, & an old foe reconcil'd.

—

Calamity and Prosperity are the Touchstones of Integrity.

—

Do me the Favour to deny me at once.

—

Don't overload Gratitude; if you do, she'll kick.

—

Don't value a man for the Quality he is of, but for the Qualities he possesses.

—

Eyes and Priests bear no Jests.

—

Fish & Visitors stink in 3 days.

—

Friends are the true Sceptres of Princes.

—

Friendship cannot live with *Ceremony*, nor without *Civility*.

—

Friendship increases by visiting Friends, but by visiting seldom.

—

Generous Minds are all of kin.

—

Gifts burst rocks.

—

Half the Truth is often a great Lie.

Half-Hospitality opens his Doors and shuts up his
Countenance.

—

He is ill cloth'd, who is bare of Virtue.

—

He makes a Foe who makes a jest.

—

Hear no ill of a Friend, nor speak any of an Enemy.

—

If any man flatters me, I'll flatter him again; tho' he were my
best Friend.

—

If thou wouldst live long, live well; for Folly and Wickedness
shorten Life.

—

If you wou'd have Guests merry with your cheer, be so your
self, or so at least appear.

—

If you would keep your Secret from an enemy, tell it not to a
Friend.

—

If you would reap Praise you must sow the Seeds,
Gentle Words and useful Deeds.

—

In a discreet man's mouth, a publick thing is private.

—

In prosperous fortunes be modest and wise,
The greatest may fall, and the lowest may rise:
But insolent People that fall in disgrace,
Are wretched and no-body pities their Case.

—

Innocence is its own Defence.

Let all Men know thee, but no man know thee thoroughly:
Men freely ford that see the shallows.

⸺

Let the letter stay for the Post, and not the Post for the Letter.

⸺

Love your Enemies, for they tell you your Faults.

⸺

Love your Neighbour; yet don't pull down your Hedge.

⸺

Men & Melons are hard to know.

⸺

Men take more pains to mask than mend.

⸺

Most People return small Favours, acknowledge middling
ones, and repay great ones with Ingratitude.

⸺

My old Friend Berryman, oft, when alive,
Taught others Thrift; himself could never thrive:
Thus like the Whetstone, many Men are wont
To sharpen others while themselves are blunt.

⸺

Neither praise nor dispraise, till seven Christmasses be over.

⸺

No better relation than a prudent & faithful Friend.

⸺

No Resolution of Repenting hereafter, can be sincere.

⸺

None but the well-bred man knows how to confess a fault, or
acknowledge himself in an error.

⸺

Nor Eye in a letter, nor Hand in a purse, nor Ear in the secret
of another.

Nothing so popular as GOODNESS.

—

Now glad the Poor with *Christmas* Cheer;
Thank God you're able so to end the Year.

—

Promises may get thee Friends, but Nonperformance will turn
them into Enemies.

—

Speak with contempt of none, from slave to king,
The meanest Bee hath, and will use, a sting.

—

Tart Words make no Friends: a spoonful of honey will catch
more flies than Gallon of Vinegar.

—

Tell a miser he's rich, and a woman she's old, you'll get no
money of one, nor kindness of t'other.

—

Tell me my Faults, and mend your own.

—

The generous Mind least regards money, and yet most feels the
Want of it.

—

The Man of pure and simple Heart
Thro' Life disdains a double part;
He never needs the screen of Lies
His inward Bosom to disguise.

—

The Master-piece of Man, is to live to the purpose.

—

The nearest way to come at glory, is to do that for conscience
which we do for glory.

The noblest question in the world is *What Good may I do in it?*

The rotten Apple spoils his Companion.

The same man cannot be both Friend and Flatterer.

The Sun never repents of the good he does, nor does he ever demand a recompence.

The World is full of fools and faint hearts; and yet every one has courage enough to bear the misfortunes, and wisdom enough to manage the Affairs of his neighbour.

There are three faithful friends, an old wife, an old dog, and ready money.

Those who in quarrels interpose,
Must often wipe a bloody nose.

Thou canst not joke an Enemy into a Friend; but thou may'st a Friend into an Enemy.

Three things are men most liable to be cheated in, a Horse, a Wig, and a Wife.

Thus with kind Words, 'squire *Edward* chear'd his Friend:
Dear Dick! thou on my Friendship mayst depend;
I know thy Fortune is but very scant;
But, be assur'd, I'll ne'er see *Dick* in Want.
Dick's soon confin'd—his Friend, no doubt, would free him:
His Word he kept—in Want he ne'er would see him.

'Tis great Confidence in a Friend to tell him *your* Faults, greater to tell him *his*.

—

'Tis less discredit to abridge petty charges, than to stoop to petty Gettings.

—

To be humble to Superiors is Duty, to Equals Courtesy, to Inferiors Nobleness.

—

To whom thy secret thou dost tell,
To him thy freedom thou dost sell.

—

Tricks and Treachery are the Practice of Fools, that have not Wit enough to be honest.

—

Trust thy self, and another shall not betray thee.

—

Visits should be short, like a winters day,
Lest you're too troublesome hasten away.

—

What signifies your Patience, if you can't find it when you want it.

—

When a Friend deals with a Friend
Let the Bargain be clear and well penn'd,
That they may continue Friends to the End.

—

When you're good to others, you are best to yourself.

—

Write Injuries in Dust, Benefits in Marble.

Keep your eyes wide open before marriage, half shut afterwards.

Of Love and Marriage, and their After-maths.

A good Wife lost is God's gift lost.

⎯

A house without woman & Fire-light, is like a body without soul or sprite.

⎯

A Man without a Wife, is but half a Man.

⎯

An undutiful Daughter, will prove an unmanageable Wife.

⎯

As to his Wife, *John* minds *St. Paul*, He's one
That hath a Wife, and is as if he'd none.

⎯

Astrologers say,
This is a good Day,
To make Love in May.

⎯

Epitaph on a Scolding Wife by her Husband.
Here my poor *Bridget's* Corps doth lie,
She is at rest, —and so am I.

⎯

Famine, Plague, War, and an unnumber'd throng
Of Guilt-avenging Ills, to Man belong;
Is't not enough Plagues, Wars, and Famines rise
To lash our crimes, but must our Wives be wise?

⎯

Fine linnen, girls and gold so bright,
Chuse not to take by candle-light.

⎯

Good wives and good plantations are made by good husbands.

[87]

Good Women are like stars in darkest Night,
Their Virtuous Actions shining as a Light
To guide their ignorant Sex, which oft times fall,
And falling oft, turns diabolical.
Good Women sure are Angels on the Earth,
Of those good Angels we have had a Dearth;
And therefore all you Men that have good Wives,
Respect their Virtues equal with your Lives.

—

Grief often treads upon the Heels of Pleasure
Marry'd in Haste, we oft repent at Leisure;
Some by Experience find these Words misplac'd,
Marry'd at Leisure, they repent in Haste.

—

Happy's the Woing, that's not long a doing.

—

He that for sake of Drink neglects his Trade,
And spends each Night in Taverns till 'tis late,
And rises when the Sun is four hours high,
And ne'er regards his starving Family;
God in his Mercy may do much to save him,
But, woe to the poor Wife, whose Lot it is to have him.

—

He that goes far to marry, will either deceive or be deceived.

—

He that has not got a Wife, is not yet a compleat Man.

—

He that takes a wife, takes care.

—

I know not which lives more unnatural Lives,
Obeying Husbands, or commanding Wives.

I never saw an oft-transplanted tree,
Nor yet an oft-removed family,
That throve so well as those that settled be.

—

If Jack's in love, he's no judge of Jill's Beauty.

—

If *Passion* drives, let *Reason* hold the Reins.

—

If you would be loved, love and be loveable.

—

Jane, why those tears? why droops your head?
Is then your other husband dead?
Or doth a worse disgrace betide?
Hath no one since his death apply'd?

—

Kate would have *Thomas*, no one blame her can:
Tom won't have *Kate*, and who can blame the Man?

—

Keep your eyes wide open before marriage, half shut
afterwards.

—

Light-heel'd mothers make leaden-heel'd daughters.

—

Little Half-wits are wondrous pert, we find,
Scoffing and jeering on whole Womankind,
ALL false, ALL Whores, ALL this and that and t'other,
Not one Exception left, ev'n for their Mother.
But Men of Wisdom and Experience know,
That there's no greater Happiness below
Than a good Wife affords; and such there's many,
For every Man has one, the best of any.

—

Love and lordship hate companions.

[89]

Love and *Tooth-ach* have many Cures, but none infallible, except *Possession* and *Dispossession.*

Love, and be lov'd.

Love, Cough, & a Smoke, can't be well hid.

Lovers, Travellers, and Poets, will give money to be heard.

Marry above thy match, and thou'lt get a Master.

Marry your Son when you will, but your Daughter when you can.

Ne'er take a wife till thou hast a house (& a fire) to put her in.

Neither a Fortress nor a Maidenhead will hold out long after they begin to parly.

Old Batchelor would have a Wife that's wise,
Fair, rich, and young, a Maiden for his Bed;
Not proud, nor churlish, but of faultless size;
A Country Houswife in the City bred.
He's a nice Fool, and long in vain hath staid;
He should bespeak her, there's none ready made.

Old England's Laws the proudest beauty name,
When single, *Spinster,* and when married, *Dame,*
For *Housewifery* is Women's noblest Fame.
The Wisest houshold Cares to Women yield,
A large, an useful, and a grateful Field.

On his Death-bed poor Lubin lies;
His Spouse is in Despair;
With frequent Sobs, and mutual Cries,
They both express their Care.
A diff'rent Cause, says Parson Sly,
The same Effect may give;
Poor Lubin fears that he shall die;
His Wife, that he may live.

—

One good Husband is worth two good Wives; for the scarcer
things are the more they're valued.

—

Pretty and Witty,
Will wound if they hit ye.

—

Prythee isn't *Miss Cloe's* a comical Case?
She lends out her Tail, and she borrows her Face.

—

Sampson with his *strong Body*, had a *weak Head*, or he would
not have laid it in a Harlot's Lap.

—

Says *Roger* to his Wife, my dear;
The strangest piece of News I hear!
A Law, 'tis said, will quickly pass,
To purge the matrimonial Class;
Cuckolds, if any such we have here
Must to a Man be thrown i' th' River.
She smiling cry'd, My dear, you seem
Surpriz'd! *Pray han't you learn'd to swim?*

She that will eat her breakfast in her bed,
And spend the morn in dressing of her head,
And sit at dinner like a maiden bride,
And talk of nothing all day but of pride;
God in his mercy may do much to save her,
But what a case is he in that shall have her.

—

Silks and Sattins put out the Kitchen Fire.

—

Squirrel-like she covers her back with her tail.

—

The end of Passion is the beginning of Repentance.

—

The good or ill hap of a good or ill life,
Is the good or ill choice of a good or ill wife.

—

The proof of gold is fire, the proof of woman, gold; the proof of
man, a woman.

—

The Reason, says Swift, why so few Marriages are happy, is,
because young Ladies spend their Time in making *nets,* not in
making *Cages.*

—

There are no ugly Loves, nor handsome Prisons.

—

Wedlock, as old Men note, hath likened been,
Unto a publick Crowd or common Rout;
Where those that are without would fain get in,
And those that are within would fain get out.

When Robin now three Days had married been,
And all his Friends and Neighbours gave him Joy;
This Question of his Wife he asked then,
Why till her Marriage Day she prov'd so coy?
Indeed (said he) 'twas well thou didst not yield,
For doubtless then my Purpose was to leave thee:
O Sir, I once before was so beguil'd,
And was resolv'd the next should not deceive me.

Where there is Marriage without Love, there will be Love
without Marriage.

Women are Books, and Men the Readers be,
Who sometimes in those Books Erratas see;
Yet oft the Reader's raptur'd with each Line,
Fair Print and Paper fraught with Sense divine;
Tho' some neglectful seldom care to read,
And faithful Wives no more than Bibles heed.
Are Women Books? says Hodge, then would mine were
An *Almanack,* to change her every Year.

You can bear your own Faults, and why not a Fault in your
Wife.

You cannot pluck roses without fear of thorns,
Nor enjoy a fair wife without danger of horns.

He that would rise at Court, must begin by Creeping.

A Cross-examination of the Lawyer and His Government.

A Courtier must be supple, full of Guile,
Must learn to praise, to flatter, to revile
The Good, the Bad; an Enemy, a Friend;
To give false Hopes, and on false Hopes depend.

—

A good Lawyer a bad Neighbour.

—

And now we're well secur'd by Law,
'Till the next Brother find a Flaw.

COURTS

For Gratitude there's none exceed 'em,
(Their Clients know this when they bleed 'em).
Since they who give most for their Laws,
Have most return'd and carry th' Cause.
All know, except an arrant Tony,
That Right and Wrong's meer Ceremony.
It is enough that the Law Jargon,
Gives the best Bidder the best Bargain.

—

George came to the Crown without striking a Blow.
Ah! quoth the Pretender, would I could do so.

—

God works wonders now & then;
Behold! a Lawyer, an honest Man!

—

Happy that nation, fortunate that age, whose history is not
diverting.

He that by Injury is griev'd,
And goes to Law to be reliev'd,
Is sillier than a sottish Chouse,
Who when a Thief has robb'd his House,
Applies himself to cunning Men
To help him to his Goods again:
When, all he can expect to gain,
Is but to squander more in vain.

—

He that would rise at Court, must begin by Creeping.

—

Honest Men often go to Law for their Right; when Wise Men
would sit down with the Wrong, supposing the first Loss least.

—

I know you Lawyers can, with Ease,
Twist Words and Meanings as you please;
That Language, by your Skill made pliant,
Will bend to favour ev'ry Client;
That 'tis the Fee directs the Sense
To make out either Side's Pretence:

—

Ignorance leads Men into a Party, and *Shame* keeps them
from getting out again.

—

In Rivers & bad Governments, the lightest Things swim
at top.

—

In some Countries the Course of the Courts is so tedious, and
the Expence so high, that the Remedy, *Justice,* is worse than,
Injustice, the Disease.

—

Kings & Bears often worry their keepers.

Laws like to *Cobwebs* catch small Flies,
Great ones break thro' before your eyes.

Laws *too gentle* are seldom *obeyed*; *too severe*, seldom *executed*.

Little Rogues easily become great Ones.

Mad kings and mad Bulls, are not to be held by treaties & packthread.

Necessity has no Law; I know some Attorneys of the name.

No longer virtuous no longer free; is a Maxim as true with regard to a private Person as a Common-wealth.

No workman without tools,
Nor Lawyer without Fools,
Can live by their Rules.

ON THE LAW
Nigh Neighbour to the Squire, poor Sam complain'd
Of frequent Wrongs, but no Amends he gain'd.
Each Day his Gates thrown down, his Fences broke,
And injur'd still the more, the more he spoke;
At last, resolv'd his potent Foe to awe,
A Suit against him he began in Law;
Nine happy Terms thro' all the Forms he run,
Obtain'd his Cause—had Costs—and was undone.

Robbers must exalted be,
Small ones on the Gallow-Tree,
While greater ones ascend to Thrones,
But what is that to thee or me?

﹏

Sudden Power is apt to be insolent, *Sudden Liberty* saucy; that
behaves best which has grown gradually.

﹏

The first Mistake in publick Business, is the going into it.

﹏

The Good-will of the Governed will be starv'd, if not fed by
the good Deeds of the Governors.

﹏

The greatest monarch on the proudest throne, is oblig'd to sit
upon his own arse.

﹏

The magistrate should obey the Laws, the People should obey
the Magistrate.

﹏

The royal Crown cures not the Head-ach.

﹏

There's many Men forget their proper Station,
And still are meddling with th' Administration
Of Government; that's wrong, and this is right,
And such a Law is out of Reason quite;
Thus spending too much Thought on State Affairs
The Business is neglected which is theirs.

﹏

So some fond Traveller gazing at the Stars
Slips in next Ditch and gets a dirty Arse.

﹏

To serve the Publick faithfully, and at the same time please it
entirely, is impracticable.

Two Beggars travelling along,
One blind, the other lame,
Pick'd up an Oyster on the Way
To which they both laid claim:
The Matter rose so high, that they
Resolv'd to go to Law,
As often richer Fools have done,
Who quarrel for a Straw.
A Lawyer took it strait in hand,
Who knew his Business was,
To mind nor one nor t'other side,
But make the best o' th' Cause;
As always in the Law's the Case:
So he his Judgment gave,
And Lawyer-like he thus resolv'd
What each of them should have:
Blind Plaintiff, lame Defendant, share,
The Friendly Laws impartial Care,
A Shell for him, a Shell for thee,
The Middle is the Lawyer's Fee.

Wars bring scars.

Where carcasses are, eagles will gather,
And where good laws are, much people flock thither.

Where there is Hunger, Law is not regarded; and where Law is
not regarded, there will be Hunger.

Where there's no Law, there's no Bread.

Without justice, courage is weak.

Ye Party Zealots, thus it fares with you.
When Party Rage too warmly you pursue;
Both Sides club Nonsense and impetuous Pride,
And *Folly* joins whom *Sentiments* divide.
You vent your Spleen as Monkeys when they pass,
Scratch at the mimic Monkey in the Glass,
While both are *one;* and henceforth be it known,
Fools of both Sides shall stand as Fools alone.

———

You may give a Man an Office, but you cannot give him
Discretion.

Many have quarrel'd about Religion, that never practis'd it.

Observations for the Day of Rest and all the rest.

Christianity commands us to pass by Injuries; Policy, to let them pass by us.

Different Sects like different clocks, may be all near the matter, 'tho they don't quite agree.

Does Mischief, Misconduct, & Warrings displease ye;
Think there's a Providence, 'twill make ye easy.

Fear God, and your enemies will fear you.

How many observe Christ's Birth-day! How few, his Precepts!
O! 'tis easier to keep Holidays than Commandments.

In the Affairs of this World Men are saved, not by Faith, but by the Want of it.

Keep thou from the Opportunity, and God will keep thee from the Sin.

Many have quarrel'd about Religion, that never practis'd it.

Many Princes sin with *David*, but few repent with him.

On buying a BIBLE
'Tis but a Folly to rejoice, or boast,
How small a Price thy well-bought Purchase cost.
Until thy Death, thou shalt not fully know
Whether it was a Pennyworth or no;
And, at that time, believe me, 'twill appear
Extreamly cheap, or else extreamly dear.

Rob not God, nor the Poor, lest thou ruin thyself; the Eagle snatcht a Coal from the Altar, but it fired her Nest.

Serving God is Doing Good to Man, but Praying is thought an easier Service, and therefore more generally chosen.

Some make Conscience of wearing a Hat in the Church, who make none of robbing the Altar.

Sound, and sound Doctrine, may pass through a Ram's Horn, and a Preacher, without straitening the one, or amending the other.

Talking against Religion is unchaining a Tyger; The Beast let loose may worry his Deliverer.

The Bell calls others to Church, but itself never minds the Sermon.

The painful Preacher, like a candle bright,
Consumes himself in giving others Light.

The Way to see by *Faith*, is to shut the Eye of *Reason*.

The Wiseman says, *It is a Wiseman's Part*
To keep his Tongue close Prisoner in his Heart.
If he then be a Fool whose Thought denies
There is a God, how desp'rately unwise,
How much more Fool is he whose Language shall
Proclaim in publick, *There's no God at all:*
What then are they, nay Fools in what degree
Whose Actions shall maintain 't? *Such Fools are we.*

⌒

When Knaves fall out, honest Men get their goods:
When Priests dispute, we come at the Truth.

⌒

Without Repentance none to Heav'n can go,
Yet what Repentance is few seem to know:
'Tis not to cry out *Mercy,* or to sit
And droop, or to confess that thou hast' fail'd;
'Tis to bewail the Sins thou didst commit,
And not commit those Sins thou hast bewail'd.
He that *bewails,* and not *forsakes* them too,
Confesses rather what he *means to do.*

⌒

Work as if you were to live 100 Years,
Pray as if you were to die To-morrow.

⌒

What is Serving God? 'Tis doing Good to Man.

⌒

Certainlie these things agree,
The Priest, the Lawyer, & Death all three:
Death takes both the weak and the strong.
The lawyer takes from both right and wrong,
and the priest from living and the dead has his Fee.

Ben beats his Pate,
and fancys
wit will come;
But he may knock,
there's no body at
home.

A humble offering of Wit
and Humour.

A—, they say, has Wit; for what?
For writing?—No; For writing not.

A modern Wit is one of David's Fools.

Bess brags she has *Beauty,* and can prove the same;
As how? why thus, Sir, 'tis her *puppy's* name.

Epitaph on a talkative old Maid.
Beneath this silent Stone is laid,
A noisy antiquated Maid,
Who from her Cradle talk'd 'till Death,
And ne'er before was out of Breath.
Whither she's gone we cannot tell;
For, if she talks not, she's in Hell:
If she's in Heaven, she's there unblest,
Because she hates a Place of Rest.

Forwarn'd, forearm'd, unless in the case of Cuckolds, who are
often forearm'd before warn'd.

Giles Jolt, as sleeping in his Cart he lay,
Some pilfring Villains stole his Team away;
Giles wakes and cries—What's here? a dickins, what?
Why, how now?—Am I Giles? or am I not?
If he, I've lost six Geldings, to my Smart;
If not,—odds buddikens, I've found a Cart.

Great talkers should be cropt, for they've no need of ears.

Jack eating rotten cheese, did say,
Like Sampson I my thousands slay;
I vow, quoth Roger, so you do,
And with the self-same weapon too.

⏤

Many would live by their Wits, but break for want of Stock.

⏤

Some have learnt many Tricks of sly Evasion,
Instead of Truth they use Equivocation,
And eke it out with mental Reservation,
Which to good Men is an Abomination.

⏤

Our Smith of late most wonderfully swore,
That whilst he breathed he would drink no more;
But since, I know his Meaning, for I think
He meant he would not breath whilst he did drink.

⏤

The Horse thinks one thing, and he that saddles him another.

⏤

The Tongue offends, and the Ears get the Cuffing.

⏤

The Tongue was once a Servant to the Heart,
And what is gave she freely did impart;
But now Hypocrisy is grown so strong
The Heart's become a Servant to the Tongue.

⏤

The worst wheel of the cart makes the most noise.

⏤

Three may keep a Secret, if two of them are dead.

⏤

To bear other Peoples afflictions, every one has Courage
enough, and to spare.

When Fortune fell asleep, and Hate did blind her,
Art, Fortune lost; and Ignorance did find her.
Since when, dull Ignorance with Fortune's Store
Hath been inrich'd, and Art hath still been poor.
Poets say Fortune's blind, and cannot see,
But certainly they must deceived be;
Else could it not most commonly fall out
That Fools should have and wise Men go without.

When Man and Woman die, as Poets sung,
His Heart's the last part moves, her last, the tongue.

       A *Cure* for *Poetry*,
Seven wealthy Towns contend for Homer, dead,
Thro' which the living Homer beg'd his Bread.

A Mob's a Monster: Heads enough, but no Brains.

As honest Hodge the Farmer, sow'd his Field,
Chear'd with the Hope of future Gain 'twould yield,
Two upstart Jacks in Office, proud and vain,
Come riding by, and thus insult the Swain.
You drudge, and sweat, and labour here, Old Boy,
But we the Fruit of your hard Toil enjoy.
Belike you may, *quoth Hodge,* and but your Due,
For, Gentlemen, 'tis Hemp I'm sowing now.

Ben beats his Pate, and fancys wit will come;
But he may knock, there's no body at home.

Dick told his spouse, he durst be bold to swear,
Whate'er she pray'd for, Heav'n would thwart her pray'r:
Indeed! says *Nell*, 'tis what I'm pleas'd to hear;
For now I'll pray for your long life, my dear.

——

I have already made this Paper too long for which I must crave
Pardon, not having Time to make it shorter.

——

Mankind are very odd Creatures: One Half censure what they
practice, the other half practice what they censure; the rest
always say and do as they ought.

——

Mary's mouth costs her nothing, for she never opens it but at
others expense.

——

Mirth pleaseth some, to others' 'tis offence,
Some commend plain conceit, some profound sense;
Some wish a witty Jest, some dislike that,
And most would have themselves they know not what.
Then he that would please all, and himself too,
Takes more in hand than he is like to do.

——

There's more old Drunkards than old Doctors.

——

To err is human, to repent divine, to persist devilish.

——

What's given shines,
What's receiv'd is rusty.

Advice on Chusing a Mistress

My dear Friend,

I know of no Medicine fit to diminish the violent natural
Inclinations you mention; and if I did, I think I should not com-
municate it to you. Marriage is the proper Remedy. It is the
most natural State of Man, and therefore the State in which
you are most likely to find solid Happiness. Your Reasons
against entring into it at present, appear to me not well-
founded. The cirmcumstantial Advantages you have in View
by postponing it, are not only uncertain, but they are small in
comparison with that of the Thing itself, the being *married and
settled*. It is the Man and Woman united that make the compleat human Being. Separate, she wants his Force of Body and
Strength of Reason; he, her Softness, Sensibility and acute
Discernment. Together they are more likely to succeed in the
World. A single Man has not nearly the Value he would have in
that State of Union. He is an incomplete Animal. He resembles
the odd Half of a Pair of Scissars. If you get a prudent healthy
Wife, your Industry in your Profession, with her good
Oeconomy, will be a Fortune sufficient.

But if you will not take this Counsel, and persist in thinking
a Commerce with the Sex inevitable, then I repeat my former
Advice, that in all your Amours you should *prefer old Women
to young ones*. You call this a Paradox, and demand my
Reasons. They are these:

1. Because as they have more Knowledge of the World and
their Minds are better stor'd with Observations, their
Conversation is more improving and more lastingly agreable.

2. Because when Women cease to be handsome, they study to
be good. To maintain their Influence over Men, they supply

the Diminution of Beauty by an Augmentation of Utility. They learn to do a 1000 Services small and great, and are the most tender and useful of all Friends when you are sick. Thus they continue amiable. And hence there is hardly such a thing to be found as an old Woman who is not a good Woman.

3. Because there is no hazard of Children, which irregularly produc'd may be attended with much Inconvenience.

4. Because thro' more Experience, they are more prudent and discreet in conducting an Intrigue to prevent Suspicion. The Commerce with them is therefore safer with regard to your Reputation. And with regard to theirs, if the Affair should happen to be known, considerate People might be rather inclin'd to excuse an old Woman who would kindly take care of a young Man, form his Manners by her good Counsels, and prevent his ruining his Health and Fortune among mercenary Prostitutes.

5. Because in every Animal that walks upright, the Deficiency of the Fluids that fill the Muscles appears first in the highest Part: The Face first grows lank and wrinkled; then the Neck; then the Breast and Arms; the lower Parts continuing to the last as plump as ever: So that covering all above with a Basket, and regarding only what is below the Girdle, it is impossible of two Women to know an old from a young one. And as in the dark all Cats are grey, the Pleasure of corporal Enjoyment with an old Woman is at least equal, and frequently superior, every Knack being by Practice capable of Improvement.

6. Because the Sin is less. The debauching a Virgin may be her Ruin, and make her for Life unhappy.

7. Because the Compunction is less. The having made a young Girl *miserable* may give you frequent bitter Reflections; none of which can attend the making an old Woman *happy*.

8[thly and Lastly] They are *so grateful!!* Thus much for my Paradox. But still I advise you to marry directly; being sincerely Your affectionate Friend

The Drinker's
Dictionary

'TIS AN OLD Remark, that Vice always endeavours to assume the Appearance of Virtue: Thus Covetousness calls itself Prudence; Prodigality would be thought Generosity; and so of others. This perhaps arises hence, that, Mankind naturally and universally approve Virtue in their Hearts, and detest Vice; and therefore, whenever thro' Temptation they fall into a Practice of the latter, they would if possible conceal it from themselves as well as others, under some other Name than that which properly belongs to it.

But Drunkenness is a very unfortunate Vice in this respect. It bears no kind of Similitude with any sort of Virtue, from which it might possibly borrow a Name; and is therefore reduc'd to the wretched Necessity of being express'd by distant round-about Phrases, and of perpetually varying those Phrases, as often as they come to be well understood to signify plainly that A Man is drunk.

Tho' every one may possibly recollect a Dozen at least of the Expressions us'd on this Occasion, yet I think no one who has not much frequented Taverns would imagine the number of them so great as it really is. It may therefore surprize as well as divert the sober Reader, to have the Sight of a new Piece, lately communicated to me, entitled

The Drinkers Dictionary.

A) He is Addled, He's casting up his Accounts, He's Afflicted, He's in his Airs.

B) He's Biggy, Bewitch'd, Block and Block, Boozy, Bowz'd, Been at Barbadoes, Piss'd in the Brook, Drunk as a Wheel-Barrow, Burdock'd, Buskey, Buzzey, Has Stole a Manchet out of the Brewer's Basket, His Head is full of Bees, Has been in the Bibbing Plot, Has drank more than he has bled, He's Bungey, As Drunk as a Beggar, He sees the Bears, He's kiss'd black Betty, He's had a Thump over the Head with Sampson's Jawbone, He's Bridgey.

C) He's Cat, Cagrin'd, Capable, Cramp'd, Cherubimical, Cherry Merry, Wamble Crop'd, Crack'd, Concern'd, Half Way to Concord, Has taken a Chirriping-Glass, Got Corns in his Head, A Cup to much, Coguy, Copey, He's heat his Copper, He's Crocus, Catch'd, He cuts his Capers, He's been in the Cellar, He's in his Cups, Non Compos, Cock'd, Curv'd, Cut, Chipper, Chickery, Loaded his Cart, He's been too free with the Creature, Sir Richard has taken off his Considering Cap, He's Chap-fallen,

D) He's Disguiz'd, He's got a Dish, Kill'd his Dog, Took his Drops, It is a Dark Day with him, He's a Dead Man, Has Dipp'd his Bill, He's Dagg'd, He's seen the Devil,

E) He's Prince Eugene, Enter'd, Wet both Eyes, Cock Ey'd, Got the Pole Evil, Got a brass Eye, Made an Example, He's Eat a Toad & half for Breakfast. In his Element,

F) He's Fishey, Fox'd, Fuddled, Sore Footed, Frozen, Well in for't, Owes no Man a Farthing, Fears no Man, Crump Footed, Been to France, Flush'd, Froze his Mouth, Fetter'd, Been to a Funeral, His Flag is out, Fuzl'd, Spoke with his Friend, Been at an Indian Feast.

G) He's Glad, Groatable, Gold-headed, Glaiz'd, Generous, Booz'd the Gage, As Dizzy as a Goose, Been before George, Got the Gout, a Kick in the Guts, Been with Sir John Goa, Been at Geneva, Globular, Got the Glanders.

H) Half and Half, Hardy, Top Heavy, Got by the Head, Hiddey, Got on his little Hat, Hammerish, Loose in the Hilts, Knows not the way Home, Got the Hornson, Haunted with Evil Spirits, Has Taken Hippocrates grand Elixir,

I) He's Intoxicated, Jolly, Jagg'd, Jambled, Going to Jerusalem, Jocular, Been to Jerico, Juicy.

K) He's a King, Clips the King's English, Seen the French King, The King is his Cousin, Got Kib'd Heels, Knapt, Het his Kettle.

L) He's in Liquor, Lordly, He makes Indentures with his Leggs, Well to Live, Light, Lappy, Limber,

M) He sees two Moons, Merry, Middling, Moon-Ey'd, Muddled, Seen a Flock of Moons, Maudlin, Mountous, Muddy, Rais'd his Monuments, Mellow,

N) He's eat the Cocoa Nut, Nimptopsical, Got the Night Mare,

O) He's Oil'd, Eat Opium, Smelt of an Onion, Oxycrocium, Overset,

P) He drank till he gave up his Half-Penny, Pidgeon Ey'd, Pungey, Priddy, As good conditioned as a Puppy, Has scalt his Head Pan, Been among the Philistines, In his Prosperity, He's been among the Philippians, He's contending with Pharaoh, Wasted his Paunch, He's Polite, Eat a Pudding Bagg,

Q) He's Quarrelsome,

R) He's Rocky, Raddled, Rich, Religious, Lost his Rudder, Ragged, Rais'd, Been too free with Sir Richard, Like a Rat in Trouble.

S) He's Stitch'd, Seafaring, In the Sudds, Strong, Been in the Sun, As Drunk as David's Sow, Swampt, His Skin is full, He's Steady, He's Stiff, He's burnt his Shoulder, He's got his Top Gallant Sails out, Seen the yellow Star, As Stiff as a Ring-bolt, Half Seas over, His Shoe pinches him, Staggerish, It is Star-light with him, He carries too much Sail, Stew'd Stubb'd, Soak'd, Soft, Been too free with Sir John Strawberry, He's right before the Wind with all his Studding Sails out, Has Sold his Senses.

T) He's Top'd, Tongue-ty'd, Tann'd, Tipium Grove,Double Tongu'd, Topsy Turvey, Tipsey, Has Swallow'd a Tavern Token, He's Thaw'd, He's in a Trance, He's Trammel'd,

V) He makes Virginia Fence, Valiant, Got the Indian Vapours,

W) The Malt is above the Water, He's Wise, He's Wet, He's been to the Salt Water, He's Water-soaken, He's very Weary, Out of the Way.

The Phrases in this Dictionary are not (like most of our Terms of Art) borrow'd from Foreign Languages, neither are they collected from the Writings of the Learned in our own, but gather'd wholly from the modern Tavern-Conversation of Tiplers. I do not doubt but that there are many more in use; and I was even tempted to add a new one my self under the Letter B, to wit, Brutify'd: But upon Consideration, I fear'd being guilty of Injustice to the Brute Creation, if I represented Drunkenness as a beastly Vice, since, 'tis well-known, that the Brutes are in general a very sober sort of People.

The Speech of Miss Polly Baker

A T CONNECTICUT NEAR Boston in New-England; where she was prosecuted the Fifth Time, for having a Bastard Child: Which influenced the Court to dispense with her Punishment, and induced one of her Judges to marry her the next Day.

May it please the Honourable Bench to indulge me in a few Words: I am a poor unhappy Woman, who have no Money to fee Lawyers to plead for me, being hard put to it to get a tolerable Living. I shall not trouble your Honours with long Speeches; for I have not the Presumption to expect, that you may, by any Means, be prevailed on to deviate in your Sentence from the Law, in my Favour. All I humbly hope is, That your Honours would charitably move the Governor's Goodness on my Behalf, that my Fine may be remitted. This is the Fifth Time, Gentlemen, that I have been dragg'd before your Court on the same Account; twice I have paid heavy Fines, and twice have been brought to Publick Punishment, for want of Money to pay those Fines. This may have been agreeable to the Laws, and I don't dispute it; but since Laws are sometimes unreasonable in themselves, and therefore repealed, and others bear too hard on the Subject in particular Circumstances; and therefore there is left a Power somewhat to dispense with the Execution of them; I take the Liberty to say, That I think this Law, by which I am punished, is both unreasonable in itself, and particularly severe with regard to me, who have always lived an inoffensive Life in the Neighbourhood where I was born, and defy my Enemies (if I have any) to say I ever wrong'd Man, Woman, or Child. Abstracted from the Law, I cannot conceive (may it please your Honours) what the Nature of my Offence is. I have brought Five fine Children into the World, at the Risque of my Life; I have maintain'd them well by my own Industry, without burthening the Township, and would have done it better, if it had not been for the heavy Charges and Fines I have paid. Can it be a Crime (in the Nature of Things I mean) to add to the Number of the King's Subjects, in a new Country that really wants People? I own it, I should think it a Praise-worthy, rather than a punishable Action. I have debauched no other Woman's Husband, nor enticed any Youth; these Things I never was charg'd with, nor has any one the least Cause of Complaint against me, unless, perhaps, the Minister, or Justice, because I have had Children without being married, by which they have missed a Wedding Fee. But, can ever this be a Fault of mine? I appeal to your Honours. You are pleased to allow I don't want Sense; but I must be stupified to the last Degree, not to prefer the Honourable State of Wedlock, to the Condition I have lived in. I always was, and still am willing to enter into it; and doubt not my behaving well in it, having all the Industry, Frugality, Fertility, and Skill in Oeconomy, appertaining to a good Wife's Character. I defy any Person to say, I ever refused an Offer of that Sort: On the contrary, I readily consented to the only Proposal of Marriage that ever was made me, which was when I was a Virgin; but too easily confiding in the Person's Sincerity that made it, I unhappily lost my own Honour, by trusting to his; for he got me with Child, and then forsook me: That very Person you all know; he is now become a Magistrate of this Country; and I had Hopes he would have appeared this Day on the Bench, and have endeavoured to moderate the Court in my Favour; then I should have scorn'd to have mention'd it; but I must now complain of it, as unjust and unequal, That my Betrayer and Undoer, the first Cause of all my Faults and Miscarriages (if they must be deemed such) should be advanc'd to Honour and Power in the Government, that punishes my Misfortunes with Stripes and Infamy. I should be told, 'tis like, That were there no Act of Assembly in the Case, the Precepts of Religion are violated by my Transgressions. If mine, then, is a religious Offence, leave it to religious Punishments. You have already excluded me from the Comforts of your Church-Communion. Is not that sufficient? You believe I have offended Heaven, and must suffer eternal Fire: Will not that be sufficient? What Need is there, then, of your additional Fines and Whipping? I own, I do not think as you do; for, if I thought what you call a Sin, was really such, I could not presumptuously commit it. But, how can it be believed, that Heaven is angry at my having Children, when to the little done by me towards it, God has been pleased to add his Divine Skill and admirable Workmanship in the Formation of their Bodies, and crown'd it, by furnishing them with rational and immortal Souls. Forgive me, Gentlemen, if I talk a little extravagantly on these Matters; I am no Divine, but if you, Gentlemen, must be making Laws, do not turn natural and useful Actions into Crimes, by your Prohibitions. But take into your wise Consideration, the great and growing Number of Batchelors in the Country, many of whom from the mean Fear of the Expences of a Family, have never sincerely and honourably courted a Woman in their Lives; and by their Manner of Living, leave unproduced (which is little better than Murder) Hundreds of their Posterity to the Thousandth Generation. Is not this a greater Offence against the Publick Good, than mine? Compel them, then, by Law, either to Marriage, or to pay double the Fine of Fornication every Year. What must poor young Women do, whom Custom have forbid to solicit the Men, and who cannot force themselves upon Husbands, when the Laws take no Care to provide them any; and yet severely punish them if they do their Duty without them; the Duty of the first and great Command of Nature, and of Nature's God, *Encrease and Multiply*. A Duty, from the steady Performance of which, nothing has been able to deter me; but for its Sake, I have hazarded the Loss of the Publick Esteem, and have frequently endured Publick Disgrace and Punishment; and therefore ought, in my humble Opinion, instead of a Whipping, to have a Statue erected to my Memory.

A Conclusion to *Poor Richard's Almanack*

Also by Richard Saunders

IGNORANT MEN WONDER how we Astrologers foretell the Weather so exactly, unless we deal with the old black Devil. Alas! 'tis as easy as pissing abed.

Besides the usual Things expected in an Almanack, I hope the profess'd Teachers of Mankind will excuse my scattering here and there some instructive Hints in Matters of Morality and Religion. And be not thou disturbed, O grave and sober Reader, if among the many serious Sentences in my Book, thou findest me trifling now and then, and talking idly. In all the Dishes I have hitherto cook'd for thee, there is solid Meat enough for thy Money. There are Scraps from the Table of Wisdom, that will if well digested, yield strong Nourishment to thy Mind. But squeamish Stomachs cannot eat without Pickles; which, 'tis true are good for nothing else, but they provoke an Appetite. The Vain Youth that reads my Almanack for the sake of an idle Joke, will perhaps meet with a serious Reflection, that he may ever after be the better for.